Ratio
Analysis
for
Small Business

by RICHARD SANZO

Books for Business
New York - Hong Kong

Ratio Analysis for Small Business

by
Richard Sanzo

ISBN: 0-89499-237-6

Reprinted from the 1957 edition

Books for Business
New York - Hong Kong
http://www.BusinessBooksInternational.com

Contents

About the Author

The author of *Ratio Analysis for Small Business* is Richard Sanzo, an expert on financial ratios and former Dun & Bradstreet executive. Mr. Sanzo has drawn on his many years of experience with that firm to produce this fourth edition of the work he originally wrote in 1957.

Ratio analysis is a valuable management tool for interpreting financial or operating data (from balance sheets, profit-and-loss statements, or both) to detect favorable or unfavorable trends or conditions in business performance. When used with judgment and objectivity—always keeping in mind that like any statistical technique it should be used cautiously—ratio analysis can quickly help business executives spot potential trouble spots. Applied properly the technique can be a valuable aid to sound management.

Ratio Analysis for Small Business is issued as part of the management publications program of SBA's Office of Management Information and Training.

CHAPTER 1

Control in Business Management

WHAT WOULD YOU SAY was the most significant factor in the evolution of business management over the past twenty years? Would you vote for the computer? You'd have a strong point, for, twenty years ago, the computer was just coming out of its infancy.

Only a relative handful of those earliest computers were in use, and they were used mostly for statistical and mathematical computations. Today, of course, the computer plays a wide and universal role in business, not only in sorting and organizing data, but also in controlling production, making forecasts and diverse management reports, preparing payrolls, administering credit, and controlling inventory. In fact, the computer has applications for just about every aspect of business management.

Obviously, very few small businesses own or lease computers. Nonetheless, their electronic shadows fall on many small firms in the form of monthly reports from their banks, their accountants, or as computer-prepared payrolls or accounts receivable controls. But the computer is only a tool—the manager *controls*. And it is this control over the various aspects of business which has evolved most significantly in the past two decades.

This is not meant to discount the importance of sales and

marketing administration. Nothing is more important than finding and serving a customer—as the saying goes, "Sales is the lifeblood of a business."

Sales techniques, however, haven't changed much in the last twenty years, whereas financial control methods have proliferated. Thus, from the late 1960's on, we have seen the emergence of a new executive position in top management of larger companies, the "Financial Vice-President." The position includes a variety of responsibilities, ranging from long term planning and budgeting to overseeing expenditures, from supervising accounting programs and watching over profitability to making recommendations to management on all aspects of finance. In short—*controlling*.

And again, obviously, most small businesses can't afford to hire this kind of high-powered financial manager. The small business manager must wear many hats. As one such manager put it while attending a conference of small business owners:

> When I came here, my business lost the services of its Chief Executive, Sales Manager, Controller, Advertising Department, Personnel Director, Head Bookkeeper, and Janitor.

Small business owners have to be their own financial vice-presidents, too.

For large business or small, to be successful is, first, to be controlled. A business under proper control watches carefully every dollar that comes in and every dollar that goes out and understands how its capital is to be husbanded, safeguarded, dispersed, and how to keep a portion of its profits for expansion.

Success or Failure Relates to How Management Manages

Why do tens of thousands of businesses disappear each year? Well, not only, of course, because of failure. Some owners simply decide to go into other lines of business. Others take on new associates and form new companies. Others lose interest or find they haven't got the dedication it takes.

On the other hand, an unfortunately large number are forced to close because their businesses are in the midst of bankruptcy, receivership, assignment, or reorganization under court supervision.

It's been said that more than nine out of ten business failures are caused by some weakness *in management.* This could be overstatement. If a neighborhood grocer suddenly faces competition from a new supermarket opening across the street, or the largest factory in town closes its doors throwing many people out of work, or if fires, floods, or other acts of nature devastate an area, failure can easily follow. There can always be unpredictable circumstances which adversely affect the stability of a business.

However, in most instances, failures result from either the inability of the principals to manage their affairs or mistakes in the way they handled their funds. In failure after failure, it's all too evident that the cause was ignorance, misjudgment, or other human error.

In 1975, for example, there were 11,432 businesses which went bankrupt or were otherwise insolvent. This was the largest total in eight years. These businesses owed more than $4 billion when they failed. This was by far the largest liability ever recorded for any one year—higher by 25 percent than the dollar liability figure for business failures in 1974.

By no means were these all small concerns. But, whether large or small, most of them failed because of inability to adapt to change or to *control* finances properly.

Those Who Succeed

What about the other side of the coin? What about those who make good?

Let's emphasize one thing first: business success doesn't always depend on the amount of starting capital. One of the largest and most successful building material manufacturing firms in America was started just before the Great Depression by a motivated entrepreneur with just $500. This kind of success is still possible.

Yet, because of its capital position, it's common to think that small business is always at a disadvantage. The facts argue otherwise. Sure, large business has the advantage of strong capital reserves and specialized staffs for research and promotion—but small business has the compensating advantages of simplicity and flexibility. One recalls the remarks of the president of a small western New York steel mill:

> If we get a complaint, or a customer calls us about a problem, I am in the customer's office the next morning with my sales manager and maybe one of our technical men. By the time one of our larger competitors would have begun to study the problem or appointed a committee to look into it, we have already solved the problem or taken care of the complaint and maybe walked off with another order.

But to succeed a small business must be able to use its advantages. To exploit them, the owner-manager must be:

- Competent in production and marketing
- Service minded
- Motivated and hard working
- Able to *control* financial affairs

And so, here we are back at that word—CONTROL—the key to successful management.

Small business managers usually do have a good knowledge of how to get production and sales. Indeed, they could hardly have gone into business without such capability. But many owner-managers educated in the "school of hard knocks" need to build onto that training an understanding of the following fundamentals:

- Correct allocation of expense and overhead items
- Sound credit policies and practices
- Effective inventory control, both in relation to sales and to the operating capital in the business
- Proper balance of assets, such as real estate, machinery, and equipment to capital
- Intelligent management of both current and long term liabilities
- Reasonable apportionment of earnings among competing demands, such as future growth and executive salaries

To help the business owner are two fundamental control

devices for guiding management: the balance sheet and the profit-and-loss (P & L or income) statement. Subsequent chapters will show how maximum use can be made of these devices through ratio analysis.

Business Ratios
and How They Work

A BALANCE SHEET tells how a business stands at one given moment in the business year. A profit-and-loss statement sums up the results of operations over a period of time.

Of themselves, these two types of financial documents are a collection of mute figures. But when the assorted financial symbols are interpreted and evaluated, they begin to talk.

A single balance sheet is like the opening chapters of a book—it gives the initial setting. Thus, one balance sheet will show how the capital is distributed, how much is in the various accounts, and how much surplus of assets over liabilities exists. A lone profit-and-loss statement indicates the sales volume for a given period, the amount of costs incurred, and the amount earned after allowing for all costs.

When a series of balance sheets for regularly related intervals, such as fiscal or calendar yearends, is arranged in vertical columns so that related items may be compared, the changes in these items begin to disclose trends. The comparative balance sheets are no longer snapshots, but become X-ray photos of the skeletal structure of all basic management actions and decisions.

Thus, decisions to increase basic inventories because of upward price changes may be revealed in larger quantities of merchandise on hand from one period to the next. If credits are relaxed and collections slow up when sales remain constant, there may be a successive increase in receivables. If expansion is undertaken, debts may run higher; and if losses are sustained, net worth declines.

Similarly, comparative profit-and-loss statements reveal significant changes in what took place. Were prices cut to meet competition? Then look for a lower gross profit—unless purchasing costs were reduced proportionately. Did sales go up? If so, what about expenses? Did they remain proportionate? Was more money spent on office help? Where did the money come from? How about fixed overhead? Was it controlled? It's only by comparing operating income and cost account items from one period to another that revealing answers are found.

Statements Reveal Important Relationships

In order to make comparisons meaningful, it's helpful to use relationships. If inventories are increased $50,000, for instance, the significance is difficult to evaluate unless the item is compared with sales and working capital. In other words, could the business really afford that much addition to stock? Did the merchandise turn over as fast as formerly? Or was the result an accumulation of unsalable goods? Thus, you need to relate asset and liability items to something else to make their significance easy to grasp.

Similarly, when you analyze costs in relation to sales, you can translate the cost figures into percentages of the sales. Then, by comparing the percentages from one period to another, you can see whether or not aggregate dollar totals of individual items meant progress or setbacks. Hence, profit-and-loss statements prepared by accountants show not only dollar totals, but usually also the percentages of sales represented by each item. Percentages, of course, are expressions of arithmetical proportions. *Proportions are ratios.*

Three Kinds of Ratios

Broadly speaking, there are three kinds of ratios. The first are balance sheet ratios which refer to relationships between various balance sheet items. The second are the operating ratios which show the relationships of expense items to net sales. The third group is made up of ratios which show the relationship between an item in the profit-and-loss statement and one on the balance sheet.

Ten Key Ratios

How many different ratios are significant? As might be expected, there's considerable difference of opinion on this question among experts. An early authority, Alexander Wall, while Secretary and Treasurer of Robert Morris Associates, listed 10 ratios in his book, *Basic Financial Statement Analysis*. Roy A. Foulke, another pioneer, concluded that there are 14 important ratios. On the other hand, a study by the American Society of Association Executives, made a number of years ago, found 34 separate types of financial ratios being compiled by 26 different trade associations.

That study suggested, however, that "It should be understood that the range of possible ratios is limited by the number and classification of accounts that are used in various types of business enterprises. Ratio study needs simplification . . . Ratios may lose their significance and accuracy when they become excessively detailed. . . ."

Along this line, a primary objective in this booklet was to narrow down the field of ratios to a working minimum for small business use. Because of this, selection and rejection of material have been necessary. The following ratios, for instance, reflect chiefly balance sheet relationships. A few combine balance sheet and profit and loss items, while one, net profit on net sales, is based exclusively on data from the profit and loss statement. The procedures for preparing an all-balance-sheet study follow the same pattern as those outlined for combined balance-sheet and income-statement analyses.

Against this background, then, the following 10 ratios are suggested as key ones for small business purposes:

1. Current assets to current liabilities.
2. Current liabilities to tangible net worth.

3. Net sales to tangible net worth.
4. Net sales to working capital.
5. Net profits to tangible net worth.
6. Average collection period of receivables.
7. Net sales to inventory.
8. Net fixed assets to tangible net worth.
9. Total debt to tangible net worth.
10. Net profit on net sales.

Brief definitions of these ratios appear below, followed by specific examples using data taken from the balance sheet and profit-and-loss statement on pages 11 and 17. Explanation of the terms of the financial statements used in calculating the ratio is included in the discussion of each ratio.

1. Current assets to current liabilities. Widely known as the "current ratio," this is one test of solvency, measuring the liquid assets available to meet all debts falling due within a year's time.

$$\text{Example:} \quad \frac{\text{Current assets}}{\text{current liabilities}} = \frac{\$151,468}{\$\ 76,968} = 1.97 \text{ times.}$$

Current assets are those normally expected to flow into cash in the course of a merchandising cycle. Ordinarily these include cash, notes and accounts receivable, and inventory, and at times, in addition, short term and marketable securities listed on leading exchanges at current realizable values. While some concerns may consider current items such as cash-surrender value of life insurance as current, the tendency is to treat them as noncurrent.

Current liabilities are short term obligations for the payment of cash due on demand or within a year. Such liabilities ordinarily include notes and accounts payable for merchandise, open loans payable, short term bank loans, taxes, and accruals. Other short term obligations, such as maturing equipment obligations and the like, also fall within the category of current liabilities.

Generally, it's considered advisable for a small business to maintain a current ratio of at least 2 to 1 or close to it for the sake of sound cash flow and healthy financial condition. This is not necessarily a must—particularly if a major part of the current assets are in cash and readily collectible receivables—otherwise, "2 for 1" or better is a pretty good idea.

2. Current liabilities to tangible net worth. Like the "current ratio," this is another means of evaluating financial condition by comparing what's owed to what's owned. If this ratio exceeds 80 percent, it's considered a danger sign.

$$\text{Example:} \quad \frac{\text{Current liabilities}}{\text{tangible net worth}} = \frac{\$\ 76{,}968}{\$135{,}880} = 56.6 \text{ percent.}$$

Tangible net worth is the worth of a business, minus any intangible items in the assets such as goodwill, trademarks, patents, copyrights, leaseholds, treasury stock, organization expenses, or underwriting discounts and expenses. In a corporation, the tangible net worth would consist of the sum of all outstanding capital stock—preferred and common—and surplus, minus intangibles. In a partnership or proprietorship, it could be made up of the capital account, or accounts, less the intangibles.

A word about "intangibles." In a going business, these items frequently have a great but undeterminable value. Until these intangibles are actually liquidated by sale, it is difficult for an analyst to evaluate what they might bring. In some cases, they have no commercial value except to those who hold them: for instance, an item of goodwill. To a profitable business up for sale, the goodwill conceivably could represent the potential earning power over a period of years, and actually bring more than the assets themselves. On the other hand, another business might find itself unable to realize anything at all on goodwill. Since the real value of intangible assets is frequently difficult to determine and evaluate, intangibles are customarily given little consideration in financial statement analysis.

3. Net sales to tangible net worth. Often called "turnover of tangible net worth," this ratio shows how actively invested capital is being put to work by indicating its turnover during a period. Both overwork and underwork of tangible net worth are considered unhealthy.

$$\text{Example:} \quad \frac{\text{Net sales}}{\text{tangible net worth}} = \frac{\$759{,}016}{\$135{,}880} = 5.6 \text{ times.}$$

There is no particular norm for this ratio. Each line of business tends to establish its own, according to studies made by

Figure 1

ANY SMALL BUSINESS, INC.
Balance Sheet
December 31, 19—

Assets

Current Assets:

Cash on hand and in banks		$ 17,280
Notes receivable	$19,280	
Less notes discounted	12,000	7,280
Accounts receivable	$87,780	
Less reserve for bad debts	7,500	80,280
Inventories		41,540
Prepayment of expenses		5,088
Total current assets		$151,468

Plant and equipment:

Land and building	$57,980	
Equipment, fixtures, and furniture	19,200	
Less allowances for depreciation	15,800	61,380

Intangibles:

Goodwill	2,000	
Patents	2,000	4,000
Total assets		$216,848

Liabilities

Current liabilities:

Notes payable (bank)	$ 16,000
Accounts payable (trade)	41,288
Taxes payable	14,400
Other payables	5,280
Total current liabilities	$ 76,968
Long term debt	0
Total liabilities	$ 76,968

Capital

Capital stock	$100,000	
Surplus	39,880	
Total equity or net worth		$139,880
Total liabilities and capital		$216,848

Dun & Bradstreet, Robert Morris Associates, trade associations, and others.

4. Net sales to working capital. Known, as well, as "turnover of working capital" this ratio also measures how actively the working cash in a business is being put to work in terms of sales. Working capital or cash is assets that can readily be converted into operating funds within a year. It does not include invested capital. A low ratio shows unprofitable use of working capital; a high one, vulnerability to creditors.

Example: $\dfrac{\text{Net sales}}{\text{working capital}} = \dfrac{\text{net sales}}{\text{current assets—current liabilities}}$

$$= \dfrac{\$759,016}{\$151,468\text{-}76,968} = 10.2 \text{ times.}$$

Deduct the sum of the current liabilities from the total current assets to get working capital, the business assets which can readily be converted into operating funds. A business with $900,000 in cash, receivables, and inventories and no unpaid obligations would have $900,000 in working capital. A business with $900,000 in current assets and $300,000 in current liabilities also would have $600,000 working capital. Obviously, however, items like receivables and inventories cannot usually be liquidated overnight. Hence, most businesses require a margin of current assets over and above current liabilities to provide for stock and work-in-process inventory, and also to carry ensuing receivables after the goods are sold until the receivables are collected.

The importance of maintaining an adequate amount of working capital in relation to the amount of annual sales being financed cannot be overemphasized. And it is this degree of adequacy which the ratio of net sales to working capital measures.

5. Net profits to tangible net worth. As the measure of return on investment, this is increasingly considered one of the best criteria of profitability, often the key measure of management efficiency. Profits "after taxes" are widely looked upon as the final source of payment on investment plus a source of funds available for future growth. If this "return on capital" is too low, the capital involved could be better used elsewhere.

Example: $\dfrac{\text{Net profits (after taxes)}}{\text{tangible net worth}} = \dfrac{\$ 23,768}{\$135,880} = 17.5 \text{ percent.}$

This ratio relates profits actually earned in a given length of time to the average net worth during that time. Profit here means the revenue left over from sales income and allowing for payment of all costs. These include costs of goods sold, write-downs and chargeoffs, Federal and other taxes accruing over the period covered, and whatever miscellaneous adjustments may be necessary to reduce assets to current, going values. The ratio is determined by dividing tangible net worth at a given period into net profits for a given period. The ratio is expressed as a percentage.

6. Average collection period of receivables. This ratio, known also as the "collection period" ratio, shows how long the money in a business is tied up in credit sales. In comparing this figure with net maturity in selling terms, many consider a collection period excessive if it is more than 10 to 15 days longer than those stated in selling terms. To get the collection period figure, get average daily credit sales, then divide into the sum of notes and accounts receivable.

Example: $\dfrac{\text{Net (credit sales for year)}}{\text{365 days a year}}$ = daily (credit) sales ($2,079)

Average collection period = $\dfrac{\text{notes and accounts receivable}}{\text{daily (credit) sales}}$

= $\dfrac{\$107,060}{\$\ 2,079}$ = 51.5.

This figure represents the number of days' sales tied up in trade accounts and notes receivable or the average collection received. The receivables discounted or assigned with recourse are included because they must be collected either directly by borrower, or by lender; if uncollected, they must be replaced by cash or substitute collateral. A pledge with recourse makes the borrower just as responsible for collection as though the receivables had not been assigned or discounted. Aside from this, the likely collectibility of all receivables must be analyzed, regardless of whether or not they are discounted. Hence all receivables are included in determining the average collection period.

7. Net sales to inventory. Known also as a "stock-to-sales" ratio, this hypothetical "average" inventory turnover figure is valued for purposes of comparing one company's performance with another, or with the industry's.

$$\text{Example:} \quad \frac{\text{Net sales}}{\text{inventory}} = \frac{\$759,016}{\$\ 41,540} = 18.3 \text{ times.}$$

A manufacturer's inventory is the sum of finished merchandise on hand, raw material, and material in process. It does not include supplies unless they are for sale. For retailers and wholesalers, it is simply the stock of salable goods on hand. It is expected that inventory will be valued conservatively on the basis of standard accounting methods of valuation, such as its cost or its market value, whichever is the lower.

Divide the average inventory into the net sales over a given period. This shows the number of times the inventory turned over in the period selected. It is compiled purely and only for purposes of making comparisons in this ratio from one period to another, or for other comparative purposes. This ratio is not an indicator of physical turnover. The only accurate way to obtain a physical turnover figure is to count each type of item in stock and compare it with the actual physical sales of that particular item.

Some people compute turnover by dividing the average inventory value at cost into the cost of goods sold for a particular period. However, this method still gives only an average. A hardware store stocking some 10,000 items might divide its dollar inventory total into cost of goods sold and come up with a physical average; this however, would hardly define the actual turnover of each item from paints to electrical supplies.

8. Fixed assets to tangible net worth. This ratio, which shows the relationship between investment in plant and equipment and the owner's capital, indicates how liquid net worth is. The higher this ratio, the less the owner's capital is available for use as working capital, to meet debts and payrolls, pay bills, or carry receivables.

$$\text{Example:} \quad \frac{\text{Fixed assets}}{\text{tangible net worth}} = \frac{\$\ 61,380}{\$135,880} = 45.2 \text{ percent.}$$

Fixed assets means the sum of assets such as land, buildings, leasehold improvements, fixtures, furniture, machinery, tools, and equipment, less depreciation. The ratio is obtained by dividing the depreciated fixed assets by the tangible net worth. Generally, it is inadvisable for a small business to have more than 75 percent of its tangible net worth represented by fixed assets.

9. Total debt to tangible net worth. This ratio also measures "what's owed to what's owned." As this figure approaches 100, the creditors' interest in the business assets approaches the owner's.

$$\text{Example: } \frac{\text{Total debt}}{\text{tangible net worth}} = \frac{\text{current debt} + \text{fixed debt}}{\text{tangible net worth}}$$

$$= \frac{\$\ 76,968}{\$135,880} = 56.6 \text{ percent.}$$

Total debt is the sum of all obligations owed by the company such as accounts and notes payable, bonds outstanding, and mortgages payable. The ratio is obtained by dividing the total of these debts by tangible net worth.

In this case, since there is no long term debt, the result is the same as the ratio of current liabilities to tangible net worth (item 2).

10. Net profit on net sales. This ratio measures the rate of return on net sales. The resultant percentage indicates the number of cents of each sales dollar remaining, after considering all income statement items and excluding income taxes.

A slight variation of the above occurs when net operating profit is divided by net sales. This ratio reveals the profitableness of sales—i.e., the profitableness of the regular buying, manufacturing, and selling operations of a business.

To many, a high rate of return on net sales is necessary for successful operation. This view is not always sound. To evaluate properly the significance of the ratio, consideration should be given to such factors as (1) the value of sales (2) the total capital employed and (3) the turnover of inventories and receivables. A low rate of return accompanied by rapid turnover and large sales volume, for example, may result in satisfactory earnings.

$$\text{Example: } \frac{\text{Net profits}}{\text{net sales}} = \frac{\$\ 23,768}{\$759,016} = 3.1 \text{ percent.}$$

Analyzing the Profit-and Loss (Income) Statement

Based solely on data taken from the profit-and-loss (P & L) statement, operating ratios show the percentage relationships of each item to a common base of net sales. These percentages may be compared with those of previous periods to measure a firm's performance. They also may be compared to the typical percentages of businesses in similar trades or industries when they are available. Such comparisons will indicate the competitive strengths and weaknesses of a business.

The items included in profit and loss statements vary from business to business. For example, some businesses break down their sales expense to show the costs of salesmen's salaries and commissions, advertising, delivery costs, supplies, and so forth; some do not. In the following explanation of the P & L items, only major items are included.

The following explanations briefly discuss each term in the accompanying condensed profit-and-loss statement (see page 17):

Net sales. This figure represents gross dollar sales minus merchandise returns and allowances. Some accountants also deduct cash discounts granted to customers on the theory that these are actually a reduction of the net selling price; others credit the discounts to "other" expense. "Trade" and "quantity" discounts are, of course, concessions off price, and should be deducted from the gross sales. In setting up the profit-and-loss statement in percentages, the net sales are shown as 100 percent.

Cost of goods sold. For retailers and wholesalers, this figure is the inventory at the beginning, plus purchases, plus "Freight in," and less inventory at the end of the period. "Freight out" is generally shown as delivery expense, either under separate or other sections of the statement.

For manufacturers, there are various additional items to be considered. They include supervision, power, supplies, the direct costs of manufacturing labor (including social security and unemployment taxes on factory employees), that portion of depreciation which enters into cost of production, and many others.

Gross profit on sales. This figure is obtained by deducting cost-of-goods sold from net sales.

Selling expenses. These expenses include such items as salaries of salesmen and sales executives, wages of other sales

Figure 2

ANY SMALL BUSINESS, INC.		
Condensed Profit and Loss Statement		
For year ending December 31, 19—		
Item	**Amount**	**Percent**
Gross sales	$773,888	
Less returns, allowances, and		
cash discounts	14,872	
Net sales	$759,016	100.00
Cost of goods sold	589,392	77.65
Gross profit on sales	$169,624	22.35
Selling expenses	41,916	5.52
Administrative expenses	28,010	3.69
General expenses	50,030	6.59
Financial expenses	5,248	0.69
Total expenses	125,204	16.49
Operating profit	44,420	5.86
Extraordinary expenses	1,200	0.16
Net profit before taxes	$43,220	5.70
Federal, state, and local taxes	19,542	2.56
Net profit after taxes	$23,768	3.14

employees, commissions, travel expense, entertainment expense, and advertising.

Operating profit. This is the difference between the gross profit on sales and the sum of the selling expenses.

General and administrative expenses. These expenses include officers' salaries, office overhead, light, heat, communication, salaries of general office and clerical help, cost of legal and accounting services, "fringe" taxes payable on administrative personnel, sundry types of franchise and similar taxes, and other expenses.

Financial expenses. This item would include interest, doubtful accounts, and discounts granted if not already deducted from sales.

Other operating expenses and income. Here might be included various unusual expense items not elsewhere classified, such as moving expenses, against which might be credited income from investments and miscellaneous credits and debits.

Extraordinary charges (if any). Such expenses do not occur very often, but occasionally unusual costs such as losses on sale of unused fixtures and equipment do arise.

Net profit before taxes. This figure is the profit after deducting the regular and extraordinary business charges mentioned above.

Taxes. This item includes the Federal, State, and local taxes paid by the company out of its earnings.

Net profit after taxes. This figure is the final figure showing earnings available for distribution or retention.

Figure 2 illustrates how a condensed profit-and-loss statement would be expressed, first in terms of dollars, then in terms of percentages of net sales. (Not all of the above items are shown.)

CHAPTER 3

Standard or Typical Ratios

HOW MUCH RENT should I pay? How much am I entitled to charge against income for my salary? What should it cost me for making deliveries? What's the average cost of doing business in my line? How much should I pay my sales force?

Hardly academic questions. They are asked by business owners every day, as they talk among themselves, or as they discuss business problems with association executives, bankers, and credit people.

Need for Measurements

On occasion, financing problems arise which introduce further questions. One of the most common is this one: "How much should my business earn on invested capital?" Others are: "I want to buy some machinery. Can I swing the purchase on my present capital, or should I invest more money in the business?" "My competitor's business is for sale; if I buy it, will my operating capital be enough to finance both businesses?" "How fast should my inventory turn over?" "What size reserve should I carry for bad debts?"

The availability of information by which a small business owner may measure performance is important. Indeed, yardsticks in the form of typical or standard ratios for different lines of business have caused many small entrepreneurs to make worthwhile reappraisals of their business thinking.

Some time ago, for instance, a trade association representing part of the contracting business held a meeting to discuss problems in bid pricing. A problem in bidding was placed on the table. Participants were given a set of specifications and material prices on a mythical job. The problem was to figure the costs and bid on the job at a price which would return a reasonable margin of profit.

Bids ranged from 13 to 31 percent above material costs. Meanwhile, a trained cost accountant had already predetermined that the bid margin should be 26 percent. Discussing the wide variation in the results of this exercise, an officer of the association said:

> Our people just don't have an adequate understanding of their costs. They can figure the obvious items which they handle every day, but they don't allow enough for their fixed and indirect overhead costs, which aren't recognized fully until they come to check up at the end of the year. Frankly, our membership has too little understanding of all the factors that go into making up a price. As a result, very few of them are earning a fair return. But today's study of these factors in an actual case was an eye opener. . . .

At the other end of the scale, a rapidly growing number of business owners has come to look at ratios as management tools to pinpoint conditions in their businesses which need attention.

Growth of Standard Ratio Studies

Ratio analysis is not an entirely new development. As early as 1913, the Bureau of Business Research of Harvard University conducted a study of the expenses of shoestores. Since then, many more studies have been done by various trade associations, government agencies, mercantile agencies, banks, research departments of industrial and accounting firms, and schools and universities. Recognition of the importance of good operating ratios will do more than any other present influence to standardize procedures and, thereby, to improve management results.

Sampling the Field

The first step taken by organizations in developing comparative operating ratios is to get detailed profit-and-loss statements from firms in the line of business under study. Naturally, not every concern will turn over its figures, others won't have sufficiently detailed records. And some won't have kept their records in a way that can be compared with those of most of the other concerns in the line.

Of course, if all the firms' figures were kept in the same way and all businesses in the line agreed to furnish them, there would be too much information to handle practically. To get, arrange, and interpret the results would take too much time and be too expensive.

Statisticians overcome this problem by "sampling"; that is, they get information from a random number of firms located over a wide area. The concerns chosen are picked because they are fairly typical of the line in general. Therefore, what's true of the sample can be relied on to be pretty much true of the line as a whole, although no single firm will exactly fit the "sample" firm picture that emerges.

Selecting the size of the sample and the make-up of the individual units of the sample are determined by the use of various mathematical formulas, all too involved to go into here. The important thing to remember is that, when it's done properly, sampling works and gives reliable results.

Obtaining the Figures

Once a method has been worked out for sampling the line, the next step is to select names of concerns in given random areas. These come from lists furnished by an association, from mailing lists, lists of customers, reference books, or whatever other sources are available.

The next step is to send out requests to them for detailed profit-and-loss statements as of a given date. Sometimes, the surveying organization will request that the figures be returned on its own specially prepared forms to insure uniformity and comparability.

Assembling the Results

As soon as the information begins to flow back to the statisticians, the job of assembling and compiling begins. There are several methods of doing this, all of which yield some kind of middle ground figures which try to reflect as nearly typical a result as possible. Once these middle ground figures have been determined, they are often arranged in a summary reflecting in percentages the overall situation for the concerns covered. In other cases, figures may be reported in terms of dollar averages so as to show, for example, typical dollar sales.

Often, the figures are also regrouped in terms of size categories, such as stores with sales volume of $20,000–$50,000, stores doing $50,000 to $100,000 annual volume, and so on. Or, the figures may be regrouped to show differences according to area, or city versus country, or credit versus cash sales.

Finally, the studies usually pinpoint relationships of certain key items, such as dollar amount of owner's salary, or salary per sales person, or sales per square foot, average stock turnover, and so forth.

One overall summary of a cost-of-doing-business study is shown in Figure 3.

Operating Ratios Vs. Financial Ratios

The number of sources which compile comparative balance sheet ratios is relatively small, as compared with those which conduct studies of operating ratios. Much of the information which is available relative to comparative balance sheet ratios is on larger businesses.

Branches of the federal government, such as the Federal Trade Commission and the Securities and Exchange Commis-

Figure 3

Summary of Operating Ratios of 350 High Profit Hardware Stores		Percent of sales
Net sales		100.00
Cost of goods sold		64.92
Margin		35.08
Expenses:		
Payroll and other employee expenses	16.23	
Occupancy expense	3.23	
Office supplies and postage	.40	
Advertising	1.49	
Donations	.08	
Telephone and telegraph	.24	
Bad debts	.30	
Delivery	.47	
Insurance	.66	
Taxes (other than real estate and payroll)	.46	
Interest	.61	
Depreciation (other than real estate)	.57	
Supplies	.37	
Legal and accounting expenses	.31	
Dues and subscriptions	.08	
Travel, buying, and entertainment	.19	
Unclassified expenses	.64	
Total operating expense		26.33
Net operating profit		8.75
Other income		1.65
Net profit before income taxes		10.40

Source: National Retail Hardware Association

sion, have compiled various balance-sheet ratios on large corporations, and similar studies have been made by a limited number of schools and universities. A few trade associations have supplemented their studies on operating ratios in their lines with ratios on selected balance-sheet items. Banks make private ratio studies based on their own files, and use the excellent studies prepared for them by Robert Morris Associates. The compiling of comparative financial statement ratios has also been done for many years by Dun & Bradstreet, Inc.

The primary use of financial ratios is to analyze the monetary condition of a business. They reflect its health.

Operating ratios also serve very useful purposes. One is to enable a manager to allocate, budget, and plan. Successful business management makes use of them to begin each year by designating the percentage of each sales dollar which will go to salaries, rent, travel, general administration, and so forth. With such management by forecast, a business owner can control progress and, if things go wrong, make immediate adjustments. It is a means of forcing profitability.

Secondly, by comparing percentage-to-sales ratios derived by administering costs within a business with those compiled from a cross section typical of the field, the owner-manager can get a good idea if his or her operating costs are imbalanced. Then action can be taken to eliminate the imbalances and improve profitability.

CHAPTER 4

Sources of Ratio Studies

R ATIO STUDY SOURCES generally may be classified into three
groups. First are agencies which compile data for a number
of industries as a by-product of their major function. Among the
best known of these are Dun & Bradstreet, Inc., the Robert
Morris Associates, and the Accounting Corporation of America.
Second is the large number of trade associations which, often in
conjunction with colleges or universities, compile studies of the
various trade groups and industries with which they are asso-
ciated. Third are various agencies and departments of the federal government.

In addition, a few industrial companies conduct ratio studies
in their customer lines for the benefit of their clients. Among
these are Eli Lilly, the National Cash Register Corporation, and
Eastman Kodak.

Dun & Bradstreet, Inc.

Since 1932, Dun & Bradstreet has been publishing "Key
Business Ratios" in the monthly, *Dun's Review*. These financial
ratios cover 22 retail, 32 wholesale, and 71 industrial lines of

business. Dun & Bradstreet also annually compile *Cost of Doing Business*, operating ratios extracted from data in the Internal Revenue Service's *Statistics of Income*. These are published and distributed by Dun & Bradstreet and are available from their Public Relations Department, 99 Church Street, New York, New York 10007 or at any of their branches.

The following types of businesses are covered in financial and operating ratio studies issued by Dun & Bradstreet:

Key Business Ratios

Retailing

Auto and home supplies
Children's and infants' wear stores
Clothing and furnishings, men's and
  boys'
Department stores
Discount stores
Discount stores, leased departments
Family clothing stores
Furniture stores
Gasoline service stations
Grocery stores
Hardware stores
Household appliance stores
Jewelry stores
Lumber and other building materials
  dealers
Miscellaneous general merchandise
  stores
Motor vehicle dealers
Paint, glass and wallpaper stores
Radio and television stores
Retail nurseries, lawn and garden
  supply dealers
Shoe stores
Variety stores
Women's ready-to-wear stores

Wholesaling

Air conditioning and refrigeration
  equipment and supplies
Automotive equipment
Beer, wine and alcoholic beverages
Chemicals and allied products

Clothing and accessories, women's and
  children's
Clothing and furnishings, men's and
  boys'
Commercial machines and equipment
Confectionery
Dairy products
Drugs, drug proprietaries, and sundries
Electrical appliances, TV and radio sets
Electrical apparatus and equipment
Electronic parts and equipment
Farm machinery and Equipment
Footwear
Fresh fruits and vegetables
Furniture and home furnishings
Groceries, general line
Hardware
Industrial machinery and equipment
Lumber and construction materials
Meats and meat products
Metals and minerals
Paints, varnishes, and supplies
Paper and its products
Petroleum and petroleum products
Piece goods
Plumbing and heating equipment and
  supplies
Poultry and poultry products
Scrap and waste materials
Tires and tubes
Tobacco and its products

Manufacturing and Construction

Agricultural chemicals
Airplane parts and accessories

26

Bakery products
Blast furnaces, steel works and rolling mills
Blouses and waists
Books, publishing and printing
Broad woven fabrics, cotton
Canned and preserved fruits and vegetables
Commercial printing except lithographic
Communication equipment
Concrete, gypsum and plaster products
Confectionery and related products
Construction, mining and handling machinery and equipment
Converted paper and paperboard products
Cutlery, hand tools and general hardware
Dairy products
Dresses
Drugs
Electric lighting and wiring equipment
Electric transmission and distribution equipment
Electrical industrial apparatus
Electrical work
Electronic components and accessories
Engineering, laboratory and scientific instruments
Fabricated structural metal products
Farm machinery and equipment
Footwear
Fur goods
General building contractors
General industrial machinery and equipment
Grain mill products
Heating and plumbing equipment
Heavy construction, except highway and street
Hosiery
Household appliances
Industrial chemicals

Instruments, measuring and controlling
Iron and steel foundries
Knot outerwear mills
Malt liquors
Mattresses and bedsprings
Meat packing plants
Metal stampings
Metalworking machinery and equipment
Millwork
Miscellaneous machinery, except electrical
Motor vehicle parts and accessories
Nonferrous foundries
Office and store fixtures
Office computing and accounting machines
Outerwear, children's and infants'
Paints, varnishes, lacquers and enamels
Paper mills, except building paper
Paperboard containers and boxes
Passenger car, truck and bus bodies
Petroleum refining
Plastics, materials and synthetics
Plumbing, heating and air conditioning
Sawmills and planing mills
Screw machine products
Shirts, underwear and nightwear, men's and boys'
Soap, detergents, perfumes and cosmetics
Soft drinks, bottled and canned
Special industry machinery
Suits and coats, women's and misses'
Suits, coats and overcoats, men's and boys'
Surgical, medical and dental instruments
Toys, amusement and sporting goods
Trousers, men's and boys'
Underwear and nightwear, women's and children's
Wood household furniture and upholstered
Work clothing, men's and boys'

Cost of Doing Business

Retailing

Apparel and accessories
Automotive dealers

Building materials, hardware, and farm equipment
Drug and proprietary stores
Eating and drinking places

27

Food stores
Furniture and home furnishings
Gasoline service stations
General merchandise
Liquor stores

Wholesaling

Alcoholic beverages
Drugs
Dry goods
Electrical goods
Farm products
Groceries
Hardware, plumbing and heating
  equipment
Lumber and construction materials
Machinery
Metals and minerals
Motor vehicles
Paper and its products
Petroleum and its products

Manufacturing

Apparel
Chemicals and allied products
Electrical supplies and equipment
Fabricated metal products
Food products (bakery products,
  beverage industries, canned goods,
  dairy products, grain mill products,
  meats, and sugar)
Furniture and fixtures
Leather and its products
Lumber and wood products
Machinery
Motor vehicles and equipment
Ordnance except guided missiles

Paper and allied products
Petroleum refining
Primary metal industries
Printing and publishing
Rubber and miscellaneous plastics
  products
Scientific industries
Stone, clay, and glass products
Textile mill products
Tobacco
Transportation equipment

Services, Transportation, and Communication

Advertising
Air transportation
Automobile parking, repair and service
Business services
Electrical companies and systems
Gas companies and systems
Hotels
Medical services
Motion picture production
Motion picture theaters
Personal services
Pipeline transportation
Radio and television broadcasting
Railroad transportation
Repair services
Telephone and telegraph services
Trucking and warehousing
Water supply and other sanitary services
Water transportation

Finance, Insurance, and Real Estate

Agriculture and Mining

Robert Morris Associates

Long noted among the banking fraternity for extensive work in the field of ratio compilation and analysis is Robert Morris Associates, a national association of bank loan and credit officers. Founded in 1914, this organization's size is indicated by the fact that its membership comprises more than 1,200 commercial banks. Its activities include maintenance and advancement of standards of correct credit practice.

Robert Morris Associates has developed ratio studies for over 350 lines of business as indicated below. Owners and managers of small concerns wishing further information on the availability of this material may address inquiries to the Executive Manager, Robert Morris Associates, Philadelphia National Bank Building, Philadelphia, Pennsylvania 19107. Following is a list of lines of business for which Robert Morris Associates provides ratios:

Manufacturing

Advertising displays and devices
Apparel and other finished fabric
   products:
  Canvas products
  Children's clothing
  Curtains and draperies
  Men's, youths' and boys' suits, coats
   and overcoats
  Women's dresses
  Women's suits, skirts, sportswear and
   coats
  Women's undergarments and
   sleepwear
Beverages:
  Flavoring extracts and syrups
  Malt liquors
  Wines, distilled liquor and liqueurs
Caskets and burial supplies
Chemicals and allied products:
  Drugs and medicines
  Fertilizers
  Industrial chemicals
  Paint, varnish and lacquer
  Perfumes, cosmetics and other toilet
   preparations
  Plastic materials and synthetic resins
  Soap, detergents and cleaning
   preparations
Food and kindred products:
  Bread and other bakery products
  Candy and confectionery supplies
  Canned and dried fruits and
   vegetables
  Dairy products
  Flour and other grain mill products
  Frozen fruits, fruit juices, vegetables,
   and specialties
  Meat packing
  Prepared feeds for animals and
   poultry

  Vegetable oils
Furniture and fixtures:
  Mattresses and bedsprings
  Metal household furniture
  Store, office, bar and restaurant
   fixtures
  Wood furniture—except upholstered
  Wood furniture—upholstered
Jewelry, precious metals
House furnishings
Leather and leather products:
  Footwear
  Furs
  Hats
  Men's and boys' sport clothing
  Men's work clothing
  Men's, youths' and boys' separate
   trousers
  Men's, youths' and boys' shirts, collars
   and nightwear
  Luggage and special leather products
Tanning, currying, and finishing
Lumber and wood products:
  Millwork
  Prefabricated wooden buildings and
   structural members
  Sawmills and planing mills
  Veneer, plywood, and hardwood
  Wooden boxes and containers
Machinery, equipment and
   supplies—electrical:
  Air conditioning
  Electronic components and accessories
  Equipment for public utilities and
   industrial use
Machinery, except electrical equipment:
  Ball and roller bearings
  Construction and mining machinery
   and equipment
  Farm machinery and equipment
  General industrial machinery and
   equipment

Industrial and commercial
refrigeration equipment and
complete air conditioning units
Machine shops—jobbing and repair
Machine tools and metal working
equipment
Measuring, analyzing, and controlling
instruments
Oil field machinery and equipment
Special dies and tools, die sets, jigs
and fixtures
Special industry machinery
Metal industries—primary:
Iron and steel forgings
Iron and steel foundries
Non-ferrous foundries
Metal products—fabricated (except
ordnance, machinery, and
transportation equipment):
Coating, engraving, and allied services
Cutlery, hand tools and general
hardware
Enameled iron, metal sanitary ware
and plumbing supplies
Fabricated plate ware
Fabricated structural steel
Heating equipment, except electric
Metal cans
Metal doors, sash, frames, molding
and trim
Metal stampings
Miscellaneous fabricated wire
products
Miscellaneous non-ferrous fabricated
products
Screw machine products, bolts, nuts,
screws, rivets and washers
Sheet metal work
Valves and pipe fittings, except
plumbers' brass goods

Paper and allied products:
Envelopes, stationery and paper bags
Paperboard containers and boxes
Pulp, paper and paperboard

Printing, publishing and allied
industries:
Book printing
Bookbinding, and miscellaneous
related work
Books: publishing
Commercial printing, lithographic
Newspapers: publishing and printing
Periodicals

Typesetting
Rubber and miscellaneous plastics
products:
Miscellaneous plastics products
Rubber footwear and fabricated
rubber products
Stone, clay and glass products:
Brick and structural clay tile
Concrete brick, block and other
products
Minerals and earths, ground or
otherwise treated
Pressed and blown glass and glassware
Ready-mixed concrete
Textile mill products:
Broad woven fabric—cotton, silk and
synthetic
Broad woven fabric—woolens and
worsteds
Dyeing and finishing
Hosiery—anklets—children's, men's
and boys'
Hosiery—women's—full fashioned
and seamless
Knitting—Cloth, outerwear and
underwear
Narrow fabrics and other smallwares
Yarn—cotton, silk, and synthetic
Toys, amusement, sporting and athletic
goods:
Games and toys, except dolls and
children's vehicles
Sporting and athletic goods
Transportation equipment:
Aircraft parts (except electric)
Motor vehicle parts and accessories
Motor vehicles
Ship and boat building and repairing

Wholesaling

Automotive equipment and supplies:
Automobiles and other motor vehicles
Automotive equipment
Tires and tubes
Beauty and barber supplies and
equipment
Drugs, drug proprietaries and druggists'
sundries
Electrical equipment:
Electrical supplies and apparatus
Electronic parts and supplies

Radios, refrigerators and electrical
  appliances
Flowers and florists' supplies
Food, beverages and tobacco:
  Coffee, tea and spices
  Confectionery
  Dairy products and poultry
  Fish and sea foods
  Frozen foods
  Fruits and vegetables
  General groceries
  Grains
  Meats and meat products
  Tobacco and tobacco products
  Tobacco leaf
  Wine, liquor and beer
Furniture and home furnishings:
  Floor coverings
  Furniture
General merchandise
Iron, steel, hardware and related
    products:
  Air conditioning and refrigeration
    equipment and supplies
  Hardware and paints
  Metal products
  Metal scrap
  Plumbing and heating equipment and
    supplies
  Steel warehousing
Lumber, building materials and coal:
  Building materials
  Coal and coke
  Lumber and millwork

Machinery and equipment:
  Agricultural equipment
  Heavy commercial and industrial
    machinery and equipment
  Laundry and dry cleaning equipment
    and supplies
  Mill supplies
  Professional equipment and supplies
  Restaurant and hotel supplies, fixtures
    and equipment
  Transportation equipment and
    supplies, except motor vehicles

Paper and paper products:
  Printing and writing paper
  Wrapping or coarse paper and
    products

Petroleum products:
  Fuel oil
  Petroleum products

Scrap and waste materials:
  Textile waste
Sporting goods and toys
Textile products and apparel:
  Dry goods
  Footwear
  Furs
  Men's and boys' clothing
  Women's and children's clothing
  Wool

Retailing

Aircraft
Apparel and accessories:
  Family clothing stores
  Furs
  Infants' clothing
  Men's and boys' clothing
  Shoes
  Women's ready-to-wear
Boat dealers
Books and office supplies:
  Books and stationery
  Office supplies and equipment
Building materials and hardware:
  Building materials
  Hardware stores
  Heating and plumbing equipment
    dealers
  Lumber
  Paint, glass and wallpaper stores
Cameras and photographic supplies
Department stores and general
    merchandise:
  Department stores
  Dry goods and general merchandise
Drugs
Farm and garden equipment and
    supplies:
  Cut flowers and growing plants
  Farm equipment
  Feed and seed—farm and garden
    supply
Food and beverages:
  Dairy products and milk dealers
  Groceries and meats
  Restaurants
Fuel and ice dealers:
  Fuel, except fuel oil
  Fuel oil dealers
Furniture, home furnishings and
    equipment:

Floor coverings
Furniture
Household appliances
Radio, TV, and record players
Jewelry
Liquor
Luggage and gifts
Motor vehicle dealers:
  Autos—new and used
  Gasoline service stations
  Mobile homes
  Motorcycles
  Tires, batteries, and accessories
  Trucks—new and used
Musical instruments and supplies
Road machinery equipment
Sporting goods
Vending machine operators,
  merchandise

Services

Advertising agencies
Auto repair shops
Auto and truck rental and leasing
Bowling alleys
Cable television
Car washing
Commercial research and development
  laboratories
Data processing
Direct mail advertising
Engineering and architectural services
Farm products warehousing
Funeral directors
Insurance agents and brokers
Intercity bus lines

Janitorial services
Laundries and dry cleaners
Linen supply
Local trucking
Local trucking—without storage
Long distance trucking
Motels, hotels, and tourist courts
Nursing homes
Outdoor advertising
Photographic studios
Radio broadcasting
Real estate holding companies
Refrigerated warehousing, except food
  lockers
Refuse systems
Telephone communications
Transportation on rivers and canals
Travel agencies
Television stations
Water utility companies

Contractors

Not Elsewhere Classified

Beef cattle raisers
Bituminous coal mining
Bottlers—soft drinks
Commercial feed lots
Construction, sand and gravel
Crude petroleum and natural gas
  mining
Horticultural services
Poultry, except broiler chickens
Seed companies (vegetable and garden)

Accounting Corporation of America

The Accounting Corporation of America publishes semiannually the *(Mail-Me-Monday) Barometer of Small Business.* Its data are derived as a by-product of the Accounting Corporation's accounting services to clients through the country.

The *(Mail-Me-Monday) Barometer* classifies its operating ratios for the various industry groups on the basis of gross volume. The classifications vary with the industry group but seldom exceed $300,000. The emphasis is on small business.

The ratios can be obtained from the Accounting Corporation's Research Department, 1929 First Avenue, San Diego, California 92101. Following is a list of types of business for which there are ratios:

Apparel, children's and infants
Apparel, men's specialty
Apparel, men's and women's
Apparel, women's specialty
Appliance stores
Auto parts and accessories
Bakeries
Beauty shops
Cocktail lounges
Confectionery stores
Contractors—building
Contractors—specialty
Dairies
Dentists
Doctors of medicine
Dry cleaning shops
Drug stores
Feed and seed stores
Florists
Food stores—combination
Food stores—specialty
Furniture stores
Garages
Gift and novelty stores
Hardware stores
Jewelry stores

Laundromats and hand laundries
Laundries, plant
Liquor stores
Lumber and building material
Machine shops
Meat markets
Motels
Music stores
New car dealers
Nursery and garden supplies
Paint, glass and wallpaper
Photographic supply stores
Plumbing and heating equipment
Printing shops
Professional—others
Repair services
Restaurants
Service stations
Shoe stores
Sporting goods stores
Taverns
TV radio sales and service
Transportation
Used car dealers
Variety stores

National Cash Register Company

The National Cash Register Company publishes an annual "Expenses in Retailing." This booklet examines the cost of operation in about 40 lines of business. The ratios are obtained from primary sources, most of which are trade associations. For some lines of business, the expense percentages are broken down into "controllable expense" and "fixed expense." Following is a list of businesses covered in a recent NCR study:

Apparel stores
Appliance and radio-TV dealers
Automobile dealers
Auto parts dealers
Beauty shops

Book stores
Building material dealers
Cocktail lounges
Department stores
Dry cleaners

Feed stores
Florists
Food stores
Furniture stores
Garages
Gift, novelty and souvenir stores
Hardware stores
Hotels
Jewelry stores
Laundries
Liquor stores
Mass merchandising stores
Meat markets
Men's wear stores

Motels and motor inns
Music stores
Novelty stores
Nursery and garden supply stores
Photographic studio and supply stores
Professional services
Repair services
Restaurants
Service stations
Shoe stores (family)
Sporting goods stores
Supermarkets
Transportation and service
Variety stores

The Bank of America

As a service to business owners and managers and students of small business, as well as to those thinking about starting a small firm, the Bank of America periodically issues detailed studies of problems in opening a business. These studies, published in its *Small Business Reporter*, include costs-of-doing-business ratios. They can be obtained by writing to *The Small Business Reporter*, Department 3120, P.O. Box 37000, San Francisco, California. Titles of issues in recent years include:

Apparel Stores
Auto Parts
Bars
Bicycle Stores
Book Stores
Building Maintenance Services
Independent Camera Stores
Proprietary Day Care Centers
Independent Drug Stores
Coin Operated Dry Cleaning Stores
Business Equipment Rental
Convenience Food Stores
The Handicraft Business
Health Food Stores

Home Furnishing Stores
Independent Liquor Stores
Mail Order Enterprises
Mobile Home and Recreation Dealers
Independent Pet Shops
Plant Shops
Small Job Printing Shops
Repair Services
Restaurants and Food Services
Service Stations
Sewing and Needlecraft Shops
Shoe Stores
Independent Sporting Goods
Toy and Hobby Craft Stores

Specialized Industry Sources

The most important specialized industry sources for ratio data are trade associations. In addition, however, accounting firms, trade magazines, universities, and some large companies publish ratio studies.

Trade Associations. National associations which have published ratio studies in the past include the following:

American Association of Advertising Agencies, 200 Park Avenue, New York, New York 10019

American Camping Association, Bradford Woods, Martinsville, Indiana 46151

American Meat Institute, 1600 Wilson Boulevard, Arlington, Virginia 22209

American Paper Institute, 260 Madison Avenue, New York, New York 10016

American Society of Association Executives, 1101 16th Street, N.W., Washington, D.C. 20036

American Supply Association, 221 North LaSalle Street, Chicago, Illinois 60601

Bowling Proprietors Association of America, Box 5802, Arlington, Texas 76011

Building Owners and Managers Association, International, 224 South Michigan Avenue, Chicago, Illinois 60601

Door and Hardware Institute, 1815 North Fort Meyer Drive, Suite 412, Arlington, Virginia 22209

Florists' Transworld Delivery Association/Interflora, 29200 Northwestern Highway, Southfield, Michigan 48076

Foodservice Equipment Distributors Association, 332 South Michigan Avenue, Chicago, Illinois 60604

Laundry and Cleaners Allied Trades Association, 543 Valley Road, Upper Montclair, New Jersey 07043

Material Handling Equipment Distributors Association, 104 Wilmot Road, Deerfield, Illinois 60015

Mechanical Contractors Association of America, 5530 Wisconsin Avenue, N.W., Suite 750, Washington, D.C. 20015

Menswear Retailers of America, 390 National Press Building, Washington, D.C. 20043

Motor and Equipment Manufacturers' Association, 222 Cedar Lane, Teaneck, New Jersey 07666

National American Wholesale Grocers' Association, Room 1810, 51 Madison Avenue, New York, New York 10010

National Appliance and Radio-TV Dealers Association, 318 West Randolph Street, Chicago, Illinois 60606

National Art Materials Trade Association, 182 A Boulevard, Hasbrouck Heights, New Jersey 07604

National Association of Accountants, 919 Third Avenue, New York, New York 10022

National Association of Electrical Distributors, 600 Madison Avenue, New York, New York 10022

National Association of Food Chains, 1725 Eye Street, N.W., Washington, D.C. 20006

National Association of Furniture Manufacturers, 8401 Connecticut Avenue, Suite 911, Washington, D.C. 20015

National Association of Insurance Agents, Inc., 85 John Street, New York, New York 10038

National Association of Music Merchants, Inc., 35 East Wacker Drive, Chicago, Illinois 60601

National Association of Plastics Distributors, 472 Nob Hill Lane, Devon, Pennsylvania 19333

National Association of Retail Grocers of the United States, Suite 620, 2000 Spring Road, Oak Brook, Illinois 60521

National Association of Textile and Apparel Wholesalers, Statler-Hilton Hotel, 33rd Street and Seventh Avenue, New York, New York 10001

National Association of Tobacco Distributors, 58 East 79th Street, New York, New York 10021

National Automatic Merchandising Association, 7 South Dearborn Street, Chicago, Illinois 60603

National Beer Wholesalers Association of America, 6310 North Cicero Avenue, Chicago, Illinois 60646

National Confectioners Association of the United States, 36 Wabash Avenue, Chicago, Illinois 60603

National Consumer Finance Association, 1000 16th Street, N.W., Washington, D.C. 20036

National Decorating Products Association, 9334 Dielman Industrial Drive, St. Louis, Missouri 63132

National Electrical Contractors Association, Inc., 7315 Wisconsin Avenue, 13th Floor, Washington, D.C. 20014

National Electrical Manufacturers Association, 155 East 44th Street, New York, New York 10017

National Farm and Power Equipment Dealers Association, 2340 Hampton Avenue, St. Louis, Missouri 63139

National Home Furnishings Association, 405 Merchandise Mart Plaza, Chicago, Illinois 60654

National Kitchen Cabinet Association, 334 East Broadway, Louisville, Kentucky 40202

National Lumber and Building Material Dealers Association, 1990 M Street, N.W., Washington, D.C. 20036

National Machine Tool Builders Association, 7901 Westpark Drive, McLean, Virginia 22101

National Office Products Association, 1500 Wilson Boulevard, Arlington, Virginia 22209

National Oil Jobbers Council, Inc., 1750 New York Avenue, N.W., Washington, D.C. 20006

National Paint and Coatings Association, 1500 Rhode Island Avenue, N.W., Washington, D.C. 20005

National Paper Box Association, 231 Kings Highway East, Haddonfield, New Jersey 08033

National Paper Trade Association, Inc., 420 Lexington Avenue, New York, New York 10017

National Parking Association, 1101 17th Street, N.W., Washington, D.C. 20036

National Restaurant Association, One IBM Plaza, Suite 2600, Chicago, Illinois 60611

National Retail Hardware Association, 964 North Pennsylvania Avenue, Indianapolis, Indiana 46204

National Retail Merchants Association, 100 West 31st Street, New York, New York 10001

National Shoe Retailers Association, 200 Madison Avenue, New York, New York 10016

National Soft Drink Association, 1101 16th Street, N.W., Washington, D.C. 20036

National Sporting Goods Association, 717 Michigan Avenue, Chicago, Illinois 60611

National Tire Dealers and Retreaders Association, 1343 L Street, N.W., Washington, D.C. 20005

National Wholesale Druggists' Association, 670 White Plains Road, Scarsdale, New York 10583

National Wholesale Hardware Association, 1900 Arch Street, Philadelphia, Pennsylvania 19103

National Wholesale Jewelers Association, 1900 Arch Street, Philadelphia, Pennsylvania 19103

Northamerican Heating and Airconditioning Wholesalers Association, 1661 West Henderson Road, Columbus, Ohio 43220

North American Wholesale Lumber Association, Inc., Box 713, Clifton, New Jersey 07013

Northeastern Retail Lumbermens Association, 339 East Avenue, Rochester, New York 14604

Optical Wholesalers Association, 6935 Wisconsin Avenue, Washington, D.C. 20015

Painting and Decorating Contractors of America, 7223 Lee Highway, Falls Church, Virginia 22046

Petroleum Equipment Institute, 1579 East 21st Street, Tulsa, Oklahoma 74114

Printing Industries of America, Inc., 1730 North Lynn Street, Arlington, Virginia 22209

Scientific Apparatus Makers Association, 1140 Connecticut Avenue, N.W., Washington, D.C. 20036

Shoe Service Institute of America, 222 West Adams Street, Chicago, Illinois 60606

Society of the Plastics Industry, Inc., The, 355 Lexington Avenue, New York, New York 10017

Super Market Institute, Inc., 303 East Ohio Street, Chicago, Illinois 60611

United Fresh Fruit and Vegetable Association, 1019 19th Street, N.W., Washington, D.C. 20036

Urban Land Institute, 1200 18th Street, N.W., Washington, D.C. 20036

Wine and Spirit Wholesalers of America, Inc., 7750 Clayton Road, Suite 201, St. Louis, Missouri 63117

Government Sources

Federal government publications provide a wealth of data covering somewhat broader industry classifications in most cases than the private sources.

Among these are the Federal Trade Commission, the Interstate Commerce Commission, the United States Department of Commerce, the United States Department of Agriculture, the Civil Aeronautics Board, the Federal Communications Commission, the Federal Power Commission, and—notably—the Securities and Exchange Commission.

The Internal Revenue Service of the United States Treasury Department annually publishes *Statistics of Income.* This volume contains income statement and balance sheet data compiled from U.S. income tax returns.

Finally, the *Census of Business*, published at five year intervals by the Bureau of the Census, provides limited ratio and dollar financial information.

Other Sources

A number of accounting and management consulting firms have done or are doing ratio studies in selected lines of business.

Such work has been done in the hotel, restaurant, home furnishings, laundry and dry cleaning industries. In addition, various trade publications conduct ratio studies from time to time.

Two well-known industrial companies, the Eli Lilly Company (drugs) and the Eastman Kodak Company (photography) are particularly noted for their data on retail operations in their industries.

CHAPTER 5

Ratio Analysis in Action:
A Case History

R ATIOS HAVE MANY USES. They are useful in analyzing collections, in checking inventory positions, in giving guidance as
to condition of finances, in comparing expense items, and in
pinpointing potential or actual disproportions as reflected by
balance sheets and profit-and-loss statements. Later on, in a
following chapter, there will be discussion of some broad principles and applications of ratio analysis.

Sometimes, however, it is easier to develop an understanding
of application of broad principles when they are highlighted by a
concrete example. For this reason, the following case is included
to show the manner in which the use of financial and operating
ratios influenced an actual business in improving its earnings
and finances.

A Case History

Here is the story of the Middleville Lumber and Building
Supply Company. Middleville is not the company's real name.
Neither are the names of the towns, nor the names of the people.
But the following account is accurate, if fictionalized.

As the scene opens, Dave Jenkins, the proprietor of Middleville Lumber and Building Supply Company, a local retail lumberyard, is in the outer office of the president of the local bank. He is waiting to discuss renewal of a matured bank loan. At least, that is his minimum objective. What Dave really wants is to obtain from the banker an *increase* in his line of credit. At the moment, Dave is attempting to marshal some telling arguments which would accomplish such a mission.

Dave had opened the yard about 20 years ago. He knew building materials. Margins had been good, and as fast as lumber came in it was shipped out. There had been little need to worry about competition. Meanwhile, the town had been growing—and as builders put up new houses and stores, Dave's firm had profited. Dave's net worth had grown from year to year.

But lately things had been getting tight. There had been strong competition. Builders were asking concessions, and the Middleville company was hungry for new accounts. While branching out into adjoining territories, Dave had been cutting prices. Year by year, he was increasing his sales, but lately was not making much of a profit.

The bank had been helpful. It discounted his trade notes receivable, at the same time opening up a modest line of unsecured credit on his own signature. Somehow, through, word was getting around that "Dave Jenkins wasn't always meeting his bills to suppliers on time." In some cases, overdue bills were resulting in rather pointed reminders from the creditors.

In preparation for his meeting with his banker, Dave had mailed his financial statement and profit-and-loss figures to the bank. These, he knew, would be posted and compared, after which he would be called in to discuss the figures and make new arrangements. He owed the bank $18,800 of which $14,000 was on open note, already due.

Dave had written down on a sheet of paper the details of his balance sheet and operating statements. (See Figure 4, page 41.)

As Jenkins gave these figures one last going over, Roy Tompkins, the president of the bank, opened the door and called him in.

Tompkins' special interest was borderline accounts. Through a judicious loan policy and sound advice, he had aided a number of the local businessmen to stay on their feet. A file drawer in the

Figure 4

Middleville Lumber and Building Supply Company
December 31, 19—
BALANCE SHEET

Cash	$ 1,896	Notes payable, bank	$ 14,000
Notes receivable	4,876	Notes receivable, discounted	4,842
Accounts receivable	97,456	Accounts payable	152,240
Inventory	156,822	Accruals	5,440
Total current assets	$261,050	Total current liabilities	$176,522
Land and buildings	46,258	Mortgage	10,000
Equipment and fixtures	11,458	Total liabilities	$186,522
Prepaid expenses	1,278	Net worth	133,522
Total assets	$320,044	Total liabilities and net worth	$320,044

INCOME STATEMENT

	Dollars	Percent
Net sales	$727,116	100.0
Cost of goods sold	582,420	80.1
Gross Profit on sales	$144,696	19.9
Expenses:		
Drawings	$14,544	2.0
Wages	74,166	10.2
Delivery expense	10,099	1.4
Bad debts allowance	4,373	0.6
Communications	2,181	0.3
Depreciation allowance	4,382	0.6
Insurance	6,543	0.9
Taxes	10,907	1.5
Advertising	2,180	0.3
Interest	4,000	0.6
Other charges	8,358	1.1
Total expenses	141,733	19.5
Net profit	$ 2,963	0.4
Other income	2,179	0.3
Total net income	$ 5,142	0.7

corner of the office contained a group of folders, kept under lock and key, in which detailed records were kept.

The banker motioned to his visitor. "Come in, Dave; sit down." When Dave was seated, Tompkins opened his desk drawer and pulled out a group of sheets containing columns of figures posted in comparative form. The lumberman guessed that they were his.

"Glad you came in. I've been wanting to have a chat with you for quite a while. Dave, you're a good salesman, and you know lumber. How well do you know your own figures?"

"I don't know, Mr. Tompkins. Most of the time, I'm too busy in the yard to go into the ledgers. I leave most of the details to my bookkeeper."

The banker waited and then went on. "Let me ask you another question, Dave. Why do you insist on doing business for nothing?" Dave was startled, and he began to flush. He had been expecting to be taken to task for the overdue note, and had thought himself reasonably well fortified with reasons. But the conversation was now taking a turn for which he was unprepared.

"I'm *not* working for nothing," Dave countered. "These last 2 years have been tough. I've been building up business—you know that. Look at my history. I'm worth more than . . ."

"Wait a minute, Dave. I know what you're going to say. But just look at your figures. Last year, you netted a little over $5,000. The year before, it was $4,500 and that was before your taxes. You could have done better working for someone else. You made virtually nothing on invested capital."

"But how much *should* I have made?" Dave asked.

"You know, Dave, the amount of profit a concern 'should earn' on its capital is something of an academic question. Some say that the ratio of net profits after taxes to tangible net worth should be at least 15 percent. Some large businesses in your line expect a 21-to-23 percent return.

"I look at it this way: If you'd gone to work for someone else, and invested in high grade bonds, you could have safely earned around 8 percent in dividends. That's—let's see, $10,400—more than twice your earnings before taxes.

"Anyway, let's be practical. Your net profit on net sales this year was less than 1 percent. Your State association of lumber and building material dealers reports that its studies indicate an average return for its members of close to 4½ percent on sales.

"Maybe, Dave, you've got all the capital you're going to need," said the banker, as he spread out the Middleville company's figures over his desk. "You know, Dave, I'm convinced you have been violating three commandments of financial management."

"Now, wait a moment, Mr. Tompkins!" Dave countered. "You know as well as I do, I'll never borrow a dime I can't pay back, or buy a two-by-four I won't pay for. I'm solvent. Look at my figures. I've got assets to pay."

As Jenkins broke off, the banker picked up the figures and continued, "Don't get upset, Dave. I know you're honest, and I know your intentions. If we weren't sure about that, I wouldn't be talking to you. I'm thinking of something else. The three commandments I mentioned are: Don't overbuy, don't overtrade, don't overexpand. Now don't you agree you've done all three?"

Dave hedged. "Well—what makes you think so?"

"Look here." The banker and the lumberman drew up their chairs. "Let's start with your balance sheet. You show current assets of $261,000 and current debts of $176,000. Your current ratio is 1.48 to 1. That's dangerously close, according to your association. The average lumberyard should show—at a minimum—a ratio of 3 to 1. Other studies I've seen indicate a prevailing median current ratio of 3.4 to 1. So you look low on current ratio."

"Now take your working capital—current assets less current debts. In your case, it's about $84,000. That's the money you would have left over, if you were to suddenly pay off all debts by liquidating current assets. It's the protective cushion you need to have in carrying your receivables and inventory. Last year, your ratio of net sales to working capital was about nine times. Experience suggests to me that four times would have been about right. Take your turnover of tangible net worth; by that I mean the ratio of your $133,000 in tangible net worth to $727,000 in net sales. It was nearly five and one-half times for the year. My observation is that it should have been a little more than two and one-half times. I'm basing that comment on some 'standard' ratios I obtained for the comparison. That's why I say I think you've been overtrading."

"What does all this standard-ratio stuff mean?" Dave interjected.

"It's simple enough if you figure it out in logical order, Dave. Overtrading with finances is something like speeding in a car. At 30 miles an hour, a blowout is an inconvenience—but at 80 miles an hour?" Tompkins paused to let the point sink in.

"Look Dave—what if one of your big customers goes sour and you have to write some big receivables off as bad debts? What if prices take a quick tumble and your inventory declines in value?

What if building should suddenly come to a halt in this area because of a strike? How about your own health—what if you were to be sick? Suppose creditors demand their money?"

"Suppose . . ." and the banker smiled, "Suppose, Dave, we called your loan."

Dave glanced up quickly. "Okay, Mr. Tompkins, I see the point. How about the loan?"

"Let's think some things through first, Dave. We'll get to the loan—and we don't want to see you forced out of business. But let's understand this: a soundly operated business has the strength to sustain blowouts. Yours hasn't.

"Now let's examine this balance sheet again. Obviously, you need more cash. You have $1,900 in your balance right now. Your operating expenses last year were $142,000. That figures out to around about $12,000 a month. You have less than enough cash to meet a week's overhead. I'm inclined to feel that a firm should have enough cash to meet 2 weeks' overhead, as a minimum, and would really be better off to have enough cash to carry it for a month.

"Next think about your receivables. Your daily sales are about $2,000 on the average. Divide that into $102,000 in notes and accounts receivables on the balance sheet, and you have an average collection period of over 50 days. Not so bad. That compares favorably with a 51-day median shown for other lumberyards by typical ratio studies. At least, you're not in the banking business with your customers.

"Well, that brings us to inventory. Your company shows a relationship for net sales to inventory of—let's see, divide $727,000 in sales by $157,000 in inventory—yes, that's right—4.6 times a year. How about that inventory, Dave? Any dead-wood in there?" The bank president chuckled.

"Well, it's like this," Dave came back a little aggressively. "I took my inventory low. I wouldn't sell it outright for $28,000 more than what I valued it at. Why I've got $20,000 worth of roofers alone that are up 20 percent since I bought them. Of course, it'll take me several months to move that much, but they'll go for a good profit."

"I'm sure they will, and when they do you'll be looking for more bargains. Tell me, Dave, are you in business to make a profit as a merchandiser or as a speculator on price fluctuations?

What will happen if you guess wrong?" Then rather emphatically, "You *will* guess wrong someday, you know!"

"But Mr. Tompkins," remarked Dave, rather plaintively, "does a guy have to shut his eyes to a good buy?"

"No; not if he can afford it. You can't. You need that $20,000 right now to pay bills with, not to mention our note. My checkings show that you're past due with your note payment. Those roofers aren't arguing for you with your creditors. Let's face it, Dave. You are a perpetual overbuyer."

Rather vehemently Dave protested, "But business is a gamble!"

"So's driving an automobile, Dave; if you were taking a trip to California, you'd want to make sure your car was in good shape. You wouldn't just load up on gas and oil. You'd have a mechanic go over your car carefully—checking brakes, tires, engine, electrical system, windshield wipers, and so on. You'd watch out for overloading, too, because you know that excessive strain might cause a breakdown.

"Right now you're driving your business under an overload of items that strain your financial resources. Your current liabilities comprise 132 percent of your tangible net worth whereas a 30- to 35- percent ratio is all that most companies like yours are willing to carry. And 44 percent of tangible net worth is in fixed assets.

"That tells a story, too. I know the purchase of your yard property 2 years ago was tempting, even though we advised against it. Sure you cut your occupancy costs, but think of what you lost in discounts you couldn't take. Suppose you had invested just a fraction of that money in a lift truck. You'd have come out ahead on expense and have saved yourself some irritation and worry in the meantime."

"Gosh, Mr. Tompkins," Dave mused, "this begins to look as though I don't belong in business. Is that what you want to tell me?"

"Not at all, Dave," the banker replied, "What I've been doing is spotlighting a few disturbing facts to help clarify your thinking. You've been trying to take a quick and easy path around some roadblocks. in the process, you got lost.

"It isn't your balance sheet or your income statement that got you into trouble. Your statements are merely end products of some questionable management methods. The key to your problem, and to a possible solution, lies in your methods of merchandising. Your profit-and-loss statement makes that fairly clear.

"Let's start by making some comparisons. In this file, I have some data about businesses similar to yours to whom we have made loans. I have averaged some of them to find out what the bank thinks you should be doing.

"Take, for example, your expenses. Item by item they compare favorably with the averages in this file. Overall, your total expenses appear to be low—around 20 percent. On that basis, your net profit should be more than the average 13.5 percent shown in my file instead of 0.4 percent. Where's the difference? On the surface, it looks like your cost-of-sales is too high."

"You're absolutely right, Mr. Tompkins," said Dave. "Main thing, I guess, is the difference in profit margin. How do those businesses in your file get the prices?"

The banker gave Dave a keen glance. "Doing much business with Bromway Builders over in Elmville?"

"Sure," Dave came back, "thousands of dollars a month."

"New account, isn't it? I hear they're pretty sharp buyers."

"Yeah, they're rough," Dave admitted somewhat hesitantly. "But they're big-volume buyers."

"How much business do you do with builders and industrials, and how much with homeowners?" asked Tompkins.

"We don't bother much with that little stuff. It's a nuisance to cut and deliver a dozen pieces of two-by-four, six pieces of wallboard, and a pound of nails. We deal mostly in quantity, with contractors and industrial accounts."

There was no immediate reaction from the banker. Then he said, "They tell me you take business as much as 25 miles out of town. That would build up delivery costs, wouldn't it?"

Dave nodded.

"I also hear that you're a bear on service, that you'll deliver a half load to any one at moment's notice. I've seen your yardmen working overtime getting out deliveries. Sure, service keeps customers happy and brings in new ones. But there have to be offsetting compensations. Your trouble, as I see it, Dave, is price.

"They tell me you'd rather miss a meal than lose a sale. Some people say you sold a carload of dimension lumber to Bromway just last week for $10 a thousand above cost. That's a pretty small markup on such an item. Frankly, your competitors have been a little gleeful about it."

"But," Dave interposed, "isn't turnover an objective? Everybody is trying for volume nowadays. What about this business of 'Profits in pennies, volume in millions'?"

"It's a nice slogan, in its place," said the banker. "Many grocers can work on small margins, and their net comes out at pennies per dollar. But they move their goods daily and weekly. They aren't so likely to take inventory losses. They sell for cash, mostly. They don't have to invest very much capital in equipment. Their volume is steady. But when a company has to stock large inventories in advance of a season, has to carry receivables and so on, capital turnover can't help but slow down."

"Costs-of-doing-business seek their level in every line. They put a logical limit on how low you can price. Sure, if new methods of selling and moving goods come along—like self-service—then the reduction in overhead can be passed on to the customer. But if you sell a carload of dimension stock at 10 percent above cost, somewhere along the line a carload of other goods has to be marked up proportionately to offset your overhead loss. Either that, or you go broke."

Anxiously, Dave asked, "All right, what do you think I should do; give up?"

"No. That's the furthest thought from my mind. I don't think it's a question of quitting. You're too honest, likable, and hardworking. You know lumber and building supplies.

"Actually, what you and I have been doing is diagnosing some symptoms of sickness. Perhaps some kind of operation is in order. I've got a few suggestions which I believe will cure this patient—if you care to listen."

Dave's reply was quick, and relieved. "Sure, sure—I'll listen. What do you think we ought to do?"

The banker continued thoughtfully, "Thinking over your situation carefully last week, I came to the conclusion that only part, but an important part, of your troubles is financial. Let's tackle them first. You can use $40,000 more cash, right?"

"Right!"

"Very well," said the banker. "The immediate problem is the loan. I can't risk depositors' money by granting you a larger loan. But I think we can do some refunding. Your yard property appears to have appreciated in value enough so that we can consolidate the present mortgage and increase it $25,000. That will refund your $14,000 note and leave $11,000 cash. It means $25,000 in working capital. Now let's look elsewhere.

"Suppose you were to cut back some of that inventory—say $40,000. Could you manage without causing sales to decline as a result? If you could, it would bring you to an inventory turnover rate of about seven times. You already have some appreciation on that $20,000 lot of roofers."

This time Dave was slow to answer. As a merchant, he enjoyed being well stocked. He had been through some trying years when merchandise was better to have than money. A well-stocked yard gave him a comfortable feeling. But there *were* those bills.

Reluctantly, he came to a decision. "Yes, I guess we could."

"Well, let's leave that one for a minute," continued the banker. "I have one more operation to propose. I want you to give up that unprofitable Bromway account. It's my belief he's headed for trouble; he's working too close. And I believe one or two others on your books have got to start paying you a better price. It's a cinch they'd have to if they did business elsewhere. If they're worth keeping, they'll go along. In other words, I would like to see you slice $50,000 worth of unprofitable sales volume off your books. It seems like a sacrifice, I'm sure, but no operation is entirely painless."

That was a shocker. Jenkins had worked hard to acquire these accounts, even though the concessions forced on him had been painful.

Tompkins continued, "It means less capital turnover, but at no loss in profit. Also it means buying several thousand dollars less each month. So you might say that, in a sense, it supplies that much additional capital. Furthermore, it means carrying fewer receivables. Taken together, these items begin to get us closer to our objective."

Dave brightened a little. The picture was beginning to look more attractive. Living with a daily burden of debt had been no fun.

"Now," said the banker, "let's look at some profit prospects. It looks as if this do-it-yourself market is here to stay. It's small, package stuff, but it can be profitable. All over the country, lumberyards have shifted their operations to take advantage of consumer business. They have put in paint and hardware, renting power tools, and so on.

"Over in Elmville, Chuck Stebbins is grossing 30 percent on that type of business. He offsets delivery costs by adding service charges. His power-tool-rental income paid for his outlay the first year. That's not so small, you know. Families are outgrowing new homes as fast as they move in; it means new rooms to build, improvements to make—rumpus-rooms in basements, bedrooms in attics. A good many of these projects qualify for home improvement loans. The bank will take off your hands all that kind of paper you can get.

"This generation of homeowners is a new breed. More leisure hours are resulting in time spent building garages, patios, and repairs. When these people buy, they want two things: service and quality. They'll spend money to get them. If you look at the facts carefully, you'll spend money to get them. Actually, 65 percent of the lumber and building supply businesses now consider themselves full-service dealers. If you look at the facts carefully, you'll see that there's money to be made in the consumer business."

As Tompkins spoke, Dave was already beginning to make calculations.

The banker continued. "This whole proposition must raise a lot of questions in your mind. Don't try to settle it overnight. Why don't you go back to your office and do some figuring. Draw up a budget and work up a few plans. Find out how much business you can do with a reasonable markup. Start making adjustments on items that are too low in price. Prices are still rising in your line, and the adjustments shouldn't be too difficult.

"Then, think about attracting some consumer trade. It might well provide as much as 25 percent of your volume before the end of the summer. Plan on some advertising. The local paper will help you lay out copy and figure costs.

"We'd like to help you stay in business in spite of your present ratios. Well—what do you say?"

As he rose to leave, Dave replied, "You know, Mr. Tompkins, there's something about your approach that makes a lot of sense. Let me think the whole business through, for a few days, as I get more figures together. Then I'd like to map it out with you.

Meanwhile, could you get started on that mortgage? It would give me some breathing space."

The banker nodded and the two walked to the door. In parting Dave remarked, "I think I can work it out. Heaven knows, I hope so." Then with a smile, "Maybe I'll turn out to be a good businessman after all. Anyway, thanks for the education on those revealing ratios!"

CHAPTER 6

Evaluating and Interpreting Ratios

PUTTING RATIOS THROUGH THEIR PACES is likely to repay the time and effort many times over. Many a small business has been able to place operations on a sounder basis through examination of the relationships of margins and costs to sales, and by restoring balance to financial structure. Identification of a problem area can be made simpler with standards of attainable goals such as are provided by ratios. The first step in evaluating and interpreting ratios is establishing a point of view.

The Point of View

In comparing operating ratios for an individual concern with those of a given line of business, the business owner must realize that this comparison is made against averages. (Concede for the moment that these averages are typical; in other words, that the samples which afford the basis for the typical ratios are adequate and the compilations realistic.)

The first question, then, is this: Do you want to be just average? In this respect, the typical ratios are not par. They may include, but do not represent the performance of the least efficient and the most efficient firms in the sample. Hence the objective of the owner-manager should be to adjust operations so that they are at least as good as, but preferably better than, the typical operating ratios.

When dealing with balance-sheet ratios, the objective, again, is usually to do better than average. Here, though, the averages usually represent a boundary line of safety. A concern with all key ratios close to the proportions reflected by standard ratios for your line is not likely to get you into trouble.

A business may, of course, go below the average here or there, and from time to time. Its investment in fixed assets may be above average, for instance, but be offset by a high degree of liquidity of current assets. Or the fixed assets may be comfortably financed on a long term basis. Or again, a low rate of turnover of tangible net worth and working capital may be the result of an existing surplus of capital. Thus, a business doing $500,000 annual sales volume on a capital of $100,000 would show higher turnover, and somewhat greater financing problems, than a business doing the same volume with $200,000 in capital. The latter business could even show an above average ratio of fixed assets to tangible net worth, simply because it had not replaced its equipment with newer, more costly—but more efficient—machinery. The reverse situation, of course, could also develop.

Ratios are interrelated. That fact may be evaluated in terms of two fundamental precepts: Make money and stay solvent. They have a kinship with the three commandments of sound financial management mentioned earlier: Don't overbuy. Don't overtrade. And don't overexpand.

Interpreting Operating Ratios

The first step, of course, is to obtain whatever typical ratios are available. They need not always be absolutely up to date. Profit margins do not usually vary very widely from year to year. As a result, ratios of a few years back may be just as useful for initial comparisons as the very recent ratios which are much harder for the average small business owner to get. The objective is to set a starting point.

Once operating ratios are obtained, you will want to line them up on some sort of worksheet alongside an item-by-item column of your own results. Some combining of expense classifications may be necessary, but the major items should stand out.

Then comes the reduction of your own dollar operating figures to percents. Usually, a cost-of-doing-business survey will produce several sets of ratios, according to the dollar sales brackets, size of business, location, price class of merchandise, and similar factors. You will naturally want to make your comparisons according to the set ratios which fit your setup most closely.

After making a comparison, earmark those items in your own operating statement which appear seriously out of line with the trade average. Here, the first reaction may be to take some drastic step. However, more fitting would be a careful reflection as to the causes. You must know *why* your figures are out of line.

Selling expenses might be above average, for instance, because of special services to customers, compensated in turn by higher prices. Or a high-priced location could be compensated for by a better-than-average margin of gross profit. So each item should be considered in relation to the overall return.

Once these comparisons are analyzed, corrective steps in proportioning expenses to sales may be worked out. Such measures are not necessarily negative. Some managers may see ways to improve their showings by *adding* expenses. For example, perhaps the former advertising budget was too low. An increase might bring in more income.

In this connection, it is essential to understand some of the significant influences on major classifications of the operating statement.

Cost of Goods Sold and Gross Margin

Cost of goods sold and gross margin are definitely interrelated. Costs may, for example, appear high because the margin is too low. Cost of goods sold may be higher or lower than that shown by a typical ratio for several reasons.

One reason for higher cost of goods may be inventory writedowns. If inventories are high during a period, and closing inventories must be valued below original cost at inventory time, the closing inventory will be lower than normal and will affect cost of goods.

The cost of goods may be too high because of wasteful buying practices. In a manufacturing business, inefficient labor will affect the cost of converting raw materials into finished products, as will excessive manufacturing overhead.

Cost of goods also may seem high simply because of a comparatively low selling price. For example: If sales are $50,000 and cost of goods is $40,000, then gross profit on sales is 20 percent and cost of goods sold is 80 percent. But if gross profit were arbitrarily increased to 25 percent while cost of goods stayed the same, sales would be $53,300, and the $40,000 figure would represent only 75 percent of sales.

Gross profit, then, may rise or fall because of what affects the costs of goods sold. When your gross profit is seriously out of line with prevailing averages, it is a good idea to examine your buying costs and pricing structure. If the gross profit is higher, it may be a logical result of location, extra services, and the like, the cost of which must be offset by selling prices.

Cost of goods sold is also related to inventory valuations. If, for example, closing inventory is overvalued, gross profit will increase—and vice versa.

Operating Expenses

Wages and salaries. Labor cost is a major item among operating expenses in the profit-and-loss account. The reaction of a business owner to how others in the line are managing these expenses will be instinctive.

A number of ratio studies provide interesting supplementary data for analyzing wage-cost relationships. Some studies, for instance, show a breakdown of *sales per employee*. Other studies which do not make this breakdown may nevertheless show figures for typical dollar sales and dollar expenditures. In this event—if the number of employees is given—the ratio of dollar sales per employee may be computed and compared with figures for your own business.

The latter relationship would be particularly interesting in comparing *selling costs*. Many sales managers have now come to review selling costs with great care. An abnormally high selling cost-to-sales ratio may lead to questions about selling efficiency. A very low selling cost-to-sales ratio may make it worthwhile to find out whether the selling effort is being concentrated in skimming the cream of large volume customers, and whether a profitable segment of a sales territory represented by smaller volume buyers is being neglected.

At the same time, it is also possible that out-of-line sales costs may be due not so much to the inefficiency of the sales force as to sales and promotion methods. Many retailers have installed self-service departments in their stores as a means of improving their sales-to-cost ratios.

Owner's compensation. The salaries of management are another item worthy of analysis. In a proprietorship or partnership, for instance, it is often the practice to compute profits before allowing for any compensation to owner or owners. Whatever earnings are left, after all other deductions, represent their compensation. Some businessmen feel that every concern should be charged with the expense of a manager. The owner, they say, would have to employ an outside manager if he or she did not exercise that function. In this connection, typical operating ratios can give some insight into the size salary an owner should draw for being manager. It should, of course, be noted that some ratios are distorted to the extent that they combine corporation figures with those of partnerships and proprietorships.

When management compensation is too high as compared with the prevailing standard, it may indicate that an excessive part of profits, which should be retained for future growth, is being drained from the business. Such a procedure is really inviting trouble—for every business should create some kind of cushion, either for expansion or to meet unforeseen contingencies. Some businesses, of course, will be exceptions because they have available to them a liberal surplus of capital over their needs. Moreover, there are profitable concerns in today's highly competitive market, which are content to stand pat on their present volume of business.

In some instances, too high a ratio of management compensation to other items may suggest that the business is supporting too many principals. A store once operated by two partners might become less attractive as a business venture if, say, four or five partners were to start drawing from it.

Attention should also be called to the situation in which officer-owners of closely held corporations prefer to take their compensation as salaries rather than in dividends. This approach can have a very marked influence on the management payroll.

Advertising cost. Improperly used, of course, advertising may prove to be something less than a cure for competitive problems. The incident may be recalled of a small manufacturer of underwear who spent relatively large sums to bring its product before the public. The advertising was in good taste, and the campaign was well planned. Sales did go up. But so much capital had been laid out in publicity that the business was unable to pay its bills. It went bankrupt before earnings could catch up. The point is that advertising outlays must be subjected to careful planning just as are other costs.

Occupancy cost. Every dollar paid in rent should bring a proportionate return in income. If location costs are high in relation to sales, they should be offset by correspondingly higher prices. Many "swanky stores" located on "exclusive thoroughfares" take this principle for granted.

Perhaps the ratio of occupancy to sales may be a little misleading as the sole arbiter of whether or not rent costs are in line. While this is a useful standard for comparison, it is good to compute also the ratio of *rent to gross profit*. The latter is overlooked in most typical ratio studies, but you can compute and compare it from basic data in the studies.

Bad debt costs. Credit is an instrument of sales. The manufacturer or wholesaler who does not grant credit is a rarity. Credit granting is becoming increasingly in vogue among retailers. There's money in it. Some grocers, such as those specializing in home deliveries and high-priced items, find that through credit, they are able to obtain higher profit margins. In other instances, while the markup cannot be increased, the credit risk is offset by larger volume.

Nevertheless, the manager who becomes deliberately careless

about granting credit is asking for trouble. Faulty reasoning is all too easy. Take, for instance, the manager of a small retail business who was being swamped with orders from new credit accounts on Saturday mornings. This manager was in a quandary for fear that "If I ask them to fill our credit applications, I'll drive the customers away!"

Interpreting Balance-Sheet Ratios

Many business executives have not schooled themselves to the significance of financial balance in their business. As an operating executive, you very likely tend to concentrate on your income account in seeking ways to increase profits or reduce losses. Nevertheless, a careful review of your balance sheets is a worthwhile related procedure. A knowledge of the distribution of your assets and liabilities and an appreciation of the typical ratios for the more successful concerns in your line or area can be of great value. It is particularly so in judging whether the financial structure of your company should be altered or redesigned to improve operating performance.

If the operating statement shows signs of progress, it is easy to rationalize a bad situation, which could be corrected, by saying, "We don't have enough capital," or even "Let the creditors carry us for awhile; look at the business we give them."

All too often, slow payments are an end result of unhealthy underlying conditions that may ultimately endanger the business. You might find, for example, overstocked inventories, excessive collection periods, ill-thought-out expansion programs, or too large investments in fixed assets. In the course of the existence of most concerns there are peaks in business activity, followed by valleys. In the ensuing fluctuations in prices and sales, some unbalanced concerns are unable to make the adjustment. There is always a chance of trouble developing as the result of some unforeseen event such as the advent of new technology or a shift in style. If liabilities are heavy, real difficulties will certainly be faced. A business must have reserves for almost any emergency.

Current Assets to Current Liabilities

In the evolution of financial analysis, it early became a practice to compare current assets to current liabilities. The beginning and the end of financial analysis in those days was the expectation that a healthy business would have a margin of $2 in current assets to $1 in current debts. This, it was said, could be considered as "an infallible guide." That notion was not to last for long.

Later, there evolved a second simple comparison: the sum of the cash and receivables to the total of current liabilities.

Still later, a third modifidation in elementary analysis occurred. Some readers may recall that certain credit issuers, even bankers, upon receiving a balance sheet for credit consideration, would mentally write down the receivables to a valuation of 75 percent of the figure shown on the statement, while also mentally writing down the inventories by 50 percent. These write-downs were made on the theory that these assets were probably overstated to begin with, and that the write-down probably represented what the assets would bring under forced liquidation. Credit, if extended at all, would be granted only on the basis of the "revised" asset values.

However, experience has proved that no single ratio can possibly give a complete picture of financial condition. Other facts can be of vital significance, each telling its own story in conjunction with related ratios and conditions in the particular business.

Nevertheless, a current ratio *does* tell a story. It *is* an item of evidence. But it should be used with judgment. Sometimes the story is deceptive. A 4-to-1 ratio in a seasonal business might go down to 1.5 to 1 at the height of the season. Or it might be high because of large amounts of accumulated unsold inventory. In the apparel trades, it is always important to consider how much of a "carryover" exists from one season to the next; for instance, summer dresses on hand in the autumn. In this regard, a shoestore in Brooklyn had a current ratio of 4 to 1 largely because of a stock of $20,000 in high button shoes—which would never be sold.

A 2-to-1 current ratio is not necessarily a guarantee of sound financial condition, but it's not a bad idea to have one most of the time. Ratios below that figure occasionally prevail in the food industry, or among concerns which have exceptionally fast turnovers of receivables and inventories. Most managers will recognize that a current ratio less than 2 to 1 is a symptom of possible trouble. It's an outward sign that financial stress is occurring.

Liabilities to Tangible Net Worth

Beware of topheavy liabilities! If they do nothing else, they undermine business judgment. Managers who are worried about finding money to meet obligations are less likely to have the analytical objectivity they need to plan sound programs for their businesses.

One of the best indicators of topheavy liabilities is the relationship of liabilities to tangible net worth. A small business is unlikely to owe much in the way of term loans, debentures, or bonds. Term debts are more likely to be loans from officers. These are internal, and in the opinion of many creditors are the most dangerous kind of debt. Or they may be mortgage loans secured by real estate or equipment. If these are large, then the ratio of total debt to tangible net worth may prove significant.

How much can a concern afford to owe? Some analysts feel that for most small manufacturing concerns, a debt equivalent to 75 percent of tangible net worth is pretty high. When liabilities exceed that figure, they reason, the equity of creditors in the assets is coming too close to equaling the equity of the owners. For the small retail business, they would argue that current liabilities should seldom come to more than 50 percent of tangible net worth. Why? A retailer, they note, usually has most current assets in inventory, which must be sold to realize cash. A heavily obligated retailer may find a sudden letdown in inventory turnover embarrassing.

There are only three ways to reduce debt. *One* is to invest more capital—not always available. The *second* is to liquidate assets—not always practical. The *third* is to build up capital from earnings—not possible overnight. So watch those debts.

Turnover of Tangible Net Worth and Working Capital

When capital is forced to turn over too rapidly, a series of consequences sets in. Every dollar is tied up in some phase of operations. Every cog in the business machine has to function perfectly because there is no reserve of money which can be called upon in an emergency. There can be no letdown in orders received and in sales transacted. Receivables must be collected very promptly, and a large bad debt becomes fatal because that money was absolutely essential for paying bills.

The more a firm's inventory needs replenishment, the more rapid its rate of buying. Bills accumulate. Money has to be borrowed and these loans have to be repaid. What if there are cancellations, or strikes, or marketing changes, or if customers just stop buying? That is where liabilities begin to take on dangerous momentum.

Net Profits on Tangible Net Worth

In 1928 and 1929, radio manufacturing was tremendously profitable. One particular manufacturer made over $5 million in net profits in a single year, on an initial capital of about the same amount. A 100-percent net profit on capital in 1 year is very heady wine. Next year, the entire capital, including last year's profit, was spent in enlarging the plant. Then, the following year, the bottom fell out of radio and the company went broke.

When net profits loom large in relation to tangible net worth over a very short period, they can lead to a very warm self-appreciative glow. They are like meat to a hungry hunter, and they lure plenty of wolves out of the forests of competition.

There is not much need to belabor the issue of net profits which are too low in relation to capital.

No one has ever proved how much a concern should earn on its existing capital. Nevertheless the fact remains that business ought to make a reasonable return on the money invested in it. That return should be adequate to compensate for risk and provide incentive. After all, profit is the payoff.

Average Collection Period

Not many concerns could afford to cut off every overdue

customer. Some of these customers provide volume—and they do not all fail. A random survey of 100 concerns rated as "fair" credit risks 10 years ago would find that most of them are still in business.

Credit management implies selectivity. Credit management by rigid yardsticks is pretty cumbersome. Too lax a credit policy can turn credit into a bog, an unsafe footing for business sales. Too rigid a policy can mean loss of business and a failure to cultivate future profitable outlets.

The collection period is a medium for comparison; it doesn't pinpoint the condition of individual accounts. If the collection period is too high, it may mean deadwood in the receivables in the form of accounts that should be written off. It might even be a signal that nonbusiness receivables, such as loans to outsiders, are included. Slow collections could be a danger signal of over-dependence on too many slow payers. Too low a collection period might justify taking a few more credit risks.

So watch average collection periods—your own, and the other person's.

Inventory Turnover

One owner spent a spring vacation in the West and combined business with pleasure by buying his entire summer's require-ments from western factories. Prices were high, and he had many a happy vision of what profits would accrue from higher prices which were bound to come that summer. Apparently he never asked himself, "But what if prices go down?"

Actually, he would have been put out of business, because those commitments exceeded his capital, and he had borrowed the money with which to buy. Fortunately, prices did not decline, but they didn't go up either.

Many a marginal business has remained a live because of unexpected profits which accrued from appreciation of inven-tories in a rising market. The trouble is that sometimes those unexpected profits come to be accepted as a normal return from "astute" management. However, unexpected losses from inven-tory depreciation in a falling market have just as often become a prelude to bankruptcy for such self-acknowledged astute entre-preneurs.

An excessive inventory can result in unexpected losses from depreciation, changes in style, perishability, and price fluctuations. A typical small business will seldom find it desirable to carry more than 100 percent of its working capital in inventory.

The profits a business earns are justified by risks taken in the normal function of converting goods from raw materials to finished products, of distributing goods, of judging style and anticipating demand, of stocking goods to suit customer convenience, and of rendering services. Net profits for such functions are seldom spectacular. In other words, the legitimate function of a business is to merchandise, produce or serve—not to speculate. Speculative profits and losses are for speculators. Business owners may be entitled to speculate, if they can afford it, but they cannot afford it on creditors' money.

Fixed Assets to Tangible Net Worth

Once there was a manufacturer of what, for the sake of protecting the company, must be called "widgets." The business was started in a very small way, but the owner was quite ingenious. The widgets were unusual in that they were completely processed, whereas competing products required further operations before use. Moreover, these particular items were being produced at a comparatively low price. The demand was great. The manufacturer began to expand rapidly.

From an output of a few widgets a day, production grew until, in 2 years, it was up to 10,000 widgets a week. That was the absolute maximum; it took new machinery to accomplish that. At this point, a big customer said, "Why don't you put in an assembly line—we will take all the widgets we can get." Money was borrowed and still more machinery was installed. Production went up to 30,000 units a week. The problem was that it took all the money the owner could get to equip the new plant.

One day, the plant manager called the owner and said, "We're running low on materials. Send us more raw widgets."

The owner had to reply, "Can't—haven't any money to buy them."

Whereupon the plant's operation had to be cut back to about one-half its capacity. This was expensive because depreciation and maintenance were heavy. Payments to suppliers became very slow. Days were anxiety-filled. Only through intensive efforts was the manager able to get outsiders to recognize sufficient profit possibility to invest additional capital and put the business back on its feet. The costs of maintenance, repairs, and depreciation could have wiped out the equity.

The point to remember is that fixed-asset requirements are relative. For example, they are high for a motor carrier and a canner, low for a cotton goods converter, a wholesaler, or an average retailer. For an average small business, if fixed assets exceed 75 percent of worth, they may become unmanageable because bills cannot be paid with brick and mortar. When money is borrowed to put into fixed assets, the borrowings become a kind of mortgage on future earnings or new capital. For only earnings or new capital can repay that kind of debt. Meanwhile, maturing debt installments may become troublesome.

Management Judgment Necessary

No statistical study will substitute for management judgment. Ratios cannot give the final answer to questions of operating policy. They cannot convert every enterprise into a success overnight. They can help in measuring performance. The knowledge of what others in the same line are doing can be of real assistance in making decisions and in locating potential trouble areas. Beyond that, small business owners and managers must look to themselves for effective action.

For Further Study

THE FOLLOWING PUBLICATIONS are listed for those who may wish to explore further the many and varied aspects of ratio analysis. The list is necessarily selective in keeping with the objectives of this booklet. No discourtesy is intended toward authors whose works are not cited.

Almanac of Business and Financial Ratios, by Leo Troy. Annual, $16.00 a copy, Prentice-Hall, Inc., Englewood Cliffs, New Jersey 07632.

Barometer of Small Business. Midyear Edition. $6 a copy. Annual subscription, including 2 issues, $12.50. Accounting Corporation of America, 1929 First Avenue, San Diego, Calif. 92101. For a number of basic types of small businesses, this study gives sales volumes and trends, as well as operating ratios. For higher groups, it shows typical financial statements.

Dynamics of the Credit Decision, by Richard Sanzo, 1975. Available on request. Dun & Bradstreet, Inc., 99 Church Street, New York, New York 10007. A review of the principles underlying credit decisions, credit ratings, and the application of financial ratios.

Expenses in Retail Businesses. Published periodically. $1.75 a copy. The National Cash Register Co., Marketing Services Department, Dayton, Ohio 45409. Operating ratios give typical experiences for various lines of retail business. For many lines, there is a breakdown by size class, as well. Average ratios, according to the compiler, "should be used by the business-man according to his own experience with his specific business and its peculiar characteristics."

Key Business Ratios in 125 Lines. Annual. Single copies free on request. Dun & Bradstreet, Inc., Business Information Systems, 99 Church Street, New York, N.Y. 10007. The 14 ratios, shown in terms of medians, cover approximately 125 lines of retail, wholesale, manufacturing, and construction business.

Cost of Doing Business: Partnerships, Proprietorships. Available on request. Dun & Bradstreet, Inc., Business Information Systems, 99 Church Street, New York, N.Y. 10007. For a number of lines of retail and wholesale trade, manufacturing, construction, services, and the like, this states operating ratios (as a percent of sales) derived from representative samples of Federal income tax returns.

Practical Financial Statement Analysis, by Roy A. Foulke, 6th ed. 1968. $14.50. McGraw-Hill Book Company, Inc., 1221 Avenue of the Americas, New York, N.Y. 10036. This book describes the background, evolution, and techniques for analyzing financial statements. By tables, it shows an interquartile range of ratios for 72 lines of business activity.

Quarterly Financial Report for Manufacturing Corporations, by Federal Trade Commission-Securities and Exchange Commission. $6.40 a year. Superintendent of Documents, U.S. Government Printing Office, Washington, D.C. 20402. This continuing series of quarterly reports, based on corporation income tax returns, shows the financial characteristics and operating results for all U.S. manufacturing corporations. Reader can use data to make his own ratio analysis.

Sources of Composite Financial Data: A Bibliography, 3d ed. Members 50¢; nonmembers $1.00. The Robert Morris Associates, Research Department, Philadelphia National Bank Building, Philadelphia, Pa. 19107. Lists and annotates 90 sources for further information on "cost of doing business," operating results, and the like, for 374 industries, including manufacturing, wholesaling, retailing, and service firms.

Statement Studies. Annual. $13.50 a year. The Robert Morris Associates, Research Department, Philadelphia National Bank Building, Philadelphia, Pa. 19107. Eleven key business ratios are presented, in terms of medians, for approximately 300 different lines of business, including manufacturers, wholesalers, retailers, and services. Businesses are broken down by size class.

www.ingramcontent.com/pod-product-compliance
Lightning Source LLC
Chambersburg PA
CBHW031814190326
41518CB00006B/336